Presented to

By

On this day

You Are
Fearfully,
Wonderfully
and **Specially**
Made
My Child:
The Beginning

For the glory of God and
better future for our children

You Are **Fearfully, Wonderfully** and **Specially** Made My Child: **The Beginning**

Michael Abayomi **Alabi**

Jesus said, "Let the little children come to Me, and do not forbid them; for of such is the kingdom of heaven." And He laid His hands on them and departed from there. (Matthew 19:14-15)

DEDICATION

This book is dedicated to my precious and beautiful daughter, Justice OluwaSade Alabi, and to the memory of my loving maternal grandmother, Felicia Awero (Mama Abeokuta). Thank you for instilling in me the virtue of godliness with contentment (1 Timothy 6:6), for not letting me have my way while I was growing up, and for leaving me the legacy of prayer, prayer, and prayer. You were not a Christian in name only; you were more so by your deeds. You lived out the gospel righteously for all to see, especially for me to know and emulate. The reason I disliked you then is the same reason I love you so much today: your faith and love for the gospel of Christ.

This book is dedicated also to the memory of my four sons, Akinola Alabi, OluwaToyin Alabi, and the twins—and to every special needs child . . . and to the memory of my dear, faithful friend and brother in the Lord, Calvin Fong. I learned so much from the way you lived as well as the way you died. I really miss you!

Sade, you truly inspire, remind, and prove to me conclusively that God's love, patience, and hope—along with goodness—always triumph over evil. It's my prayer that as you journey through life you'll continue to grow in grace—God's eternal grace. I pray you'll continue to make us proud, but, more importantly, you'll continue to make the heart of God rejoice over you. I love you.

TABLE OF CONTENTS

ACKNOWLEDGEMENTS

I praise the Lord for His loving-kindness in getting this book published. It's my prayer that this book will be a blessing to as many families as possible, and, more importantly, it will glorify God's name. A hearty thank you to Jessica Nina Oluwafunmilayo Alabi, May the Lord continue to guide, uphold, and sustain you. I pray Sade will one day rise up and call you blessed (Proverbs 31:28).

Thank you so much, Stephanie Nakayama, for your abundant countless godly counsel, your devotion to the truth, and your dedication to what is honorable. Your seeking to honor God with your profession is truly admirable. May the Lord continue to use you as a conduit of His grace and blessing and richly bless you and yours.

Pastor Brain Naidoo of South Africa, you've been the conduit of God's blessing to me from day one in 2004 when we became roommates during the Shepherd's Conference at Grace Community Church in Southern California. Thank you very much for your prayers and encouraging words in person and on Facebook. Even though we are separated by the ocean, we are constantly together in prayers and supplication by God's grace regardless of the distance. May the Lord richly bless you and the family, my brother and my friend; may He constantly bless the ministry entrusted to your care for your blessings and His glory.

Thank you Paul Skibitxke Edward (Bud) for taking the time to go over the manuscript and for your godly counsel, insight, and prayers. May the Lord richly bless you and yours.

Don Fulton, I truly valued your encouraging words during the infancy stage of this book. Brother, even though we are not able to connect more often as we'd like, your friendship, prayers, and assistance are appreciated. May the Lord continue to sustain you and yours.

To all my Bible Study Fellowship (BSF) brothers in Gardena and Cypress, Southern California, I truly appreciate your encouraging words and comments and your love for the gospel. Your willingness to hold and holding my feet to the fire is very refreshing. It's an honor and a privilege to be a part of such an eclectic group of men who are dedicated to studying and applying the Word of God. May the Lord continue to guide us to be steadfast, immoveable, and always abounding in the work of the Lord (1 Corinthians 15:58).

Thank you so much, Randy Givens (a.k.a. Yemi) and Norman Canas Mcbride, for your encouraging words on Facebook and for the challenge to put my thoughts into written form. May the Lord richly bless you and yours.

Thank you very much Rebecca McCullough of the Department of Children and Family Services (DCFS). You are one of the unsung heroes out there, your dedication, love and kindness to those less fortunate is just amazing. May the Lord reward you and yours abundantly for all you did for us.

Janet Blair of (CASA) Court Appointed Special Advocate. We will always remember your love for Sade and by extension to us and all your other children. It's such a joy to see you love Sade so tenderly. Each time you see her you always bring her new toys or a token of your love. May the God of all grace continually remember your kind deeds and bless you and yours.

Thank you very much Susan Bierlich and the entire staff at Orange Coast College, Harry & Grace Steele Children's Center in

Costa Mesa, Southern California. Your dedication, determination and love in raising the next generation is just amazing. May the Lord richly reward your efforts and continually make you a blessing.

Thank you very much, Sekou Kante. Even though we never met in person, you proved to be a true friend and a brother of kindred spirit. I truly value and appreciate your sincerity and friendship. May the Lord richly reward you for your kindness and encouraging words.

Thank you very much Ryan Lewelling, Kayla Stobaugh, Jessi Wallace, Dawn Woods, Nubia Echevarria and the editorial team for your assistance, patience and support in getting this book published. May the Lord richly bless you.

To the anonymous parents and grandparents who shared their experiences and mistakes with me, I thank you for your honesty, vulnerability, and love for the gospel of our Lord and Savior Jesus Christ. May the Lord richly bless and reward you all.

To all my Facebook friends, acquaintances, and family, I thank you for your constant encouragement and devotion to our Lord and Savior Jesus Christ; may His name be forever glorified in our lives.

To Parents, Grandparents, Guardians, Foster and Adoptive Parents, and Teachers

Before you read this book to your child, be familiar with the story of creation. If you are not, please read Genesis chapters 1 and 2. As you go through this book with your sons, daughters, grandsons, granddaughters, and students, please read it prayerfully. Don't rush through this book. Use the Bible as the main background, sole authority, and template. Whenever a reference is made from the Scriptures, please close this book and dwell on the scripture. More importantly, live out the gospel truth for your offspring to see, to hear, and to apply for their good and God's glory.

The best time to bind the minds of children to the Word of God and to fully ground them in the fear and admonition of the Lord (Ephesians 6:4) is now because tomorrow may be too late. . . . The older they get, the harder it becomes. Don't underestimate the power of their minds; they know more than you give them credit for. They know you more than you think; they see you more than you think. For the sake of the gospel of our Lord and Savior Jesus Christ and for their sake, bind their minds to the Word of

God today; their tomorrows and the rest of their lives depend upon it. Don't let the world take their todays from them; otherwise, it will take their tomorrows as well. Teach them about the genesis of their lives; let them know that they are in this world, but not of this world (John 17:15–17).

What Prompted Me to Write This Book?

I'm neither a writer nor a poet, but I enjoy expressing my thoughts in written form. This project started as I was trying to find a way to teach my daughter the principle of Christian religion. Her salvation is very close to my heart. At every prayer meeting at my church, at every Bible study, and at the Bible Study Fellowship (BSF) group, my request has always been the same: the salvation of my daughter. During the 2013 Christmas celebration at my home church, Community of Faith Bible Church (CFBC) in South Gate, California, the children staged a dramatization of the birth of Christ and sang Christ-honoring songs. The plays and songs were very moving and encouraging. I wished that my daughter was part of the group but she was not old enough to participate. After the play and before the benediction, one of the pastors of the church, Bobby Scott, said that most children raised in the church do not return to the church after going to college. He followed the statement by saying, "I pray that these kids (pointing to the children) will continue to sing the praise of King Jesus 20, 30, 40 years from now. Please join me in praying for them." The co-pastor, Anthony Kidd, echoed the same concern during our Sunday evening prayer time.

Prior to this event, I was concerned about where our world was heading. After hearing these statistics of Christian children who leave the church after going off to college, I became more disturbed and concerned. I started paying more attention and being more prayerful for my daughter's future and the future of other children I know. It was during this time I came across one of the greatest and most disturbing shocks of my life. After talking to and interviewing many parents, grandparents, teachers, uncles, and aunties—and after watching their interactions with their children, grandchildren, nieces, nephews, and students—I came to the conclusion that our children do not leave the church when they go to college, but have already left the church spiritually, emotionally, and intellectually—right under our noses—while we think they are in the church. I believe this is due largely to the fact that we abdicate our responsibility as caregivers. The world is changing every day, so we must be more aware of the world in which our children live. The way we were raised must not be the way we raise them; this is a different world. We must invest our time wisely on them.

I don't want to be insensitive by overlooking the fact that there are many godly parents and grandparents, Sunday school teachers, youth leaders, and pastors out there who have spent countless years on their knees on behalf of their offspring, students, and family members who are still motivated by worldly values. I salute your perseverance in the faith. Please don't be weary; it's going to pay off if we don't give up. The good news is that it is never too late, even if they are now grown and on their own and have departed from the faith. Even if we look back and see that we weren't watchful enough while they were growing up, allowing them to be caught up in the quagmire of a world we don't approve of, we can still call them up, sit with them, and apologize for the lack of foresight. We can invest some time with them and their children; we can always redeem the time.

One of the musical groups that my daughter listens to said something that truly enrages and frightens me, but also wakes me up. This musical group is very colorful, charming, and entertaining. Their niche market is children between the ages of 2–10 years, and their concerts are always sold out. The kids (with their parents) fill the auditorium, dancing their hearts out without paying any attention to the lyrics of the songs they are listening to because this music is very colorful and danceable; it has upbeat rhythms to it . . . but the lyrics are very destructive, dangerous, and damning. This proves conclusively that everything that glitters is not gold. Please pay closer attention to and be more interested in the lyrics of the songs your children listen to—even more than rhythm or tune. (Those who have ears to hear, let them hear because time is of the essence.)

Here's a sample of the lyrics this musical group sings to the children:

> Nobody knows you better than you,
> Nobody does you better than you,
> Nobody loves you better than you,
> We'll do it our way.

Upon listening to these lyrics, my mind almost went into a rage. It went back to the genesis of life, back to the garden of Eden, back to the temptation of Eve by the devil (Genesis 3:1–7; 1 John 2:16). The doubt, distrust, autonomous living, self-empowerment, and discouragement that the devil planted into the mind of Eve—that same doubt, distrust, autonomous living, self-empowerment, and discouragement is now being planted into our children's minds. If nobody knows you better than you, nobody does you better than you, and nobody loves you better than you, then the most natural, logical, and reasonable conclusion is for you to do it your way because you know best and you love best. This constitutes making man more supreme than God. Doubt and distrust of their parents' love is now being planted in their unschooled minds; even more devastating, doubt and distrust of the love of God is being planted in their minds as they are being discreetly encouraged to challenge His (God's) love for them. If Adam and Eve did not survive this assault from the devil in a plush, beautiful, and sinless garden, how can these children ever survive it in a not-so-glorious environment full of sin? Before we become alarmed and distraught that children leave the church after going to college, we need to realize that the seeds of distrust, doubt, and even hatred of the church have been planted deep in their hearts at a very early age.

Before you take your child to an event or any activity, you might want to ask yourself the following questions taken from the book *Right Thinking in a World Gone Wrong* by Pastor John MacArthur.[1]

1. Will this activity produce spiritual benefit? (1 Corinthians 10:23)
2. Will this activity lead to spiritual bondage? (1 Corinthians 6:12)
3. Will this activity expose my mind or body to defilement? (1 Corinthians 6:19–20)
4. Will this activity benefit others, or cause them to stumble? (1 Corinthians 8:9)
5. Will this activity further the cause of the gospel? (1 Corinthians 9:19–23; 10:32–33)
6. Will this activity violate my conscience? (Romans 14:23)
7. Will this activity bring glory to God? (1 Corinthians 10:31)

Consider the following questions, and seriously think about them: Am I part of the problem or part of the solution? What impact will this event or activity have on them (my child or children) for the rest of their lives? Will this activity or event lead to eternal life? Will where I'm taking them become an eternal snare to their soul and their path to godliness? If my child (or children) turns out to be just like me, will they be worldly or godly? If all children were just like my child or children, what type of world would this be? If all future Christian children turn out just like my child or children, what will Christendom become? How effectively does my Christ-honoring lifestyle draw my offspring to Him?

I know that in this new age in which we live, "compromise" and "tolerance" are the operative words for politically correct social interaction. Will you compromise your faith in the face of opposition? It was Joe Carter who said, "We may be required to tolerate ungodly behavior, but the moment we begin to endorse it, we too become suppressors of the truth. You cannot love your neighbor and want to see them excluded from the kingdom of Christ."

At the age of two, my daughter was taught, "Jesus loves me, this I know, for the Bible tells me so." She can even sign it, which brings so much joy and hope to my heart and mind. Whenever we eat, she always clasps her hands and repeats the simple table grace after us: "God is good, God is great, and we thank Him for this food. Bow our heads, we are fed, thank You, Lord, for our daily bread. In Jesus' name, amen." To see her clasp her little hands for prayer every morning and every night makes my heart flow with so much joy. At the age of two she began to repeat after us whatever we said. She began to sing along and even know by heart the theme songs of the cartoons we showed her. Her first lesson in theology was God, and rightly so.

Question: What is your name?
Answer: OluwaSade.
Question: Who made Sade?
Answer: God.
Question: What did God make?
Answer: Everything.

This godly beginning brings so much joy to my heart and mind. I know full well that by God's grace she will continue to build on this legacy and knowledge, thereby growing in His grace.

We bought Sade the CD and DVD of the above-mentioned group due to their colorful appearance and popularity.. We watched them with her, but—to my amazement—after a couple of times watching this DVD and listening to the CD, she began to sing along with them. She even began to demand to watch this band (whose lyrics I quoted above), crying hysterically whenever her demand was not obliged. Then it became very clear in my mind that the world will do anything and everything to capture children's hearts and minds before we realize it, thereby implanting in them erroneous doctrines totally antithetical to the right and truthful way of life and living as prescribed by their Maker—God. Hence, when they go off to college, all restraints are totally off. They are now free to exhibit the full content of their hearts and minds that has been restrained and repressed while they were at home, going to church with us, their parents.

The upbringing and religious education of our children are not the sole responsibility of the school system, teachers, big brothers or sisters, Boy or Girl Scouts, youth leaders, the state, or the nation. Yes, all these groups of people may contribute to their upbringing inasmuch as their contribution is based on the faith once given to the saints (Jude 3). The ultimate responsibilities of raising the kids are the parents'—especially the father's, as ordained by God (Ephesians 6:4). We fathers must realize that we have a huge responsibility to safeguard our family members, especially the most vulnerable— our children. We are God's expression of love to our families; we are the rock of the family, the umbrella, the gatekeeper, the priest, the provider, the protector, and everything in between. We represent our heavenly Father to our earthly children. May the Lord grant us the grace to represent Him in the way He ought to be represented.

We need to realize the fact that we are at war with the culture, and it's a war that can only be won on bended knees. We need to be aware of the erosion of their souls; as parents, we must start their growth in God's grace from the genesis of their lives. There's an African proverb that states, "A river that forgets its source will dry out." So it is with our children; they must always be reminded that their source of life and living is God and God alone. To forget God is to lose their source of life and living; hence, they will dry out.

The world around our children is not leaving any stone unturned; they are starting to reach them right from the beginning of their lives. If possible, they would start their pernicious scheme right from the womb. We need to be mindful of the fact that the devil is constantly seeking those whom he may devour (1 Peter 5:8). Our children's minds are always flooded with subliminal messages that even many adults cannot handle. "They are a lot safer if they never taste the fruit of error than to taste it even as we try to stop them." The destructive words being fed to them do not just stay on their minds, but they go deep into their hearts; that is where the destruction begins. Once these words pass through the grid of the mind to the heart, then the war begins to rage. Solomon clearly warned us to guard our heart with all diligence, for out of it flow the issues of life (Proverbs 4:23).

We need to realize that there is a connection between the function of faith and declaration of faith. It's about time we think seriously and meditate on that amazing hymn titled "Christian, Seek Not Yet Repose" as written by Charlotte Elliott in 1836—one hundred seventy-eight years ago (the music was composed by William H. Monk in 1868). This song is as applicable today as it was then. The refrain must be on our minds every day so we know where our victory lies: by watching and praying.

Christian, Seek Not Yet Repose

Verse 1
Christian, seek not yet repose;
Hear Thy guardian angel say
Thou art in the midst of foes:
Watch and pray.

Verse 2
Principalities and power
Mustering their unseen array
Wait for thy unguarded hours:
Watch and pray.

Verse 3
Gird thy heavenly armour on;
Wear it ever, night and day;
Ambushed lies the evil one;
Watch and pray.

Verse 4
Hear the victors who overcame;
Still they mark each warrior's way;
All with one sweet voice exclaim,
Watch and pray.

Verse 5
Hear, above all, hear the Lord,
Him thou lovest to obey;
Hide within thy heart His word:
Watch and pray.

Verse 6
Watch, as if on that alone
Hung the issue of the day:
Pray, that help may be sent down:
Watch and pray.

The main thesis of the Apostle Peter's letter to the church is to prepare us for suffering and to warn us that the antichrists are coming. "But there were also false prophets among the people, even as there will be false teachers among you, who will secretly bring in destructive heresies, even denying the Lord who bought them, and bring on themselves swift destruction" (2 Peter 2:1). The apostle John in his epistle, and Jude in his letter, say that the antichrists are already here. "Little children, it is the last hour; and as you have heard that the Antichrist is coming, even now many antichrists have come, by which we know that it is the last hour" (1 John 2:18); "For certain men have crept in unnoticed, who long ago were marked out for this condemnation, ungodly men, who turn the grace of our God into lewdness and deny the only Lord God and our Lord Jesus Christ" (Jude 4). We need to be aware and realize that the most vulnerable in our society are the children, and the assault on their hearts and minds—and the battle for their minds and souls—is now being intensified. It was Norman Geisler who said that you cannot beware of something until you are aware of it. Are you aware of the world your children are living in? Are you aware of their state of mind, the company they move with, their habits, traits, character, and so forth? We need to be alert and truly watch and pray. The days of playing church must be over now, as we remember that every word of God, as spoken and written, will not return to Him void, but will accomplish all the intended purposes as ordained by God (Isaiah 55:11). We must bear in mind that the same sun that melts the wax also hardens the clay. Let us learn from the twelve disciples of our Savior, who all heard the same Word from the same Lord and Master, ate the same food, slept under the same roof, did everything together . . . yet the Word that purified the other eleven and made them more Christlike—this same Word actually hardened Judas's heart to the end of his time. So it is with us: if the Word of God does not make you more like Christ, then it is hardening your heart. Going to church just to be with Christians can be damaging and dangerous to your soul if you are not saved and don't have any affinity for being saved. Your children see you and know you more than you think, and they will someday emulate you by just going through the motions too unless they're redeemed and saved by grace.

> *Out of the mouth of infants and babes*
> *He ordained praise.*
> *(see Psalm 8:2; Matthew 21:16)*

The Story of Fred the Rooster

I have been the recipient of God's grace by being blessed with a godly maternal grandmother who made sure that reading, under-standing, and applying Scripture is the most important thing into which I invest my time and energy. And I am even more blessed to have the joy of knowing and listening to great theologians, teachers, and preachers of the gospel of our time and times past. Men who have invested their time, energy, and lives into my life by clearly teaching, preaching, and writing about the unvarnished, true Word of God include Pastors John MacArthur, R.C. Sproul, Alistair Begg, and Rev. Ken Jones, just to mention a few. To whom much is given, much is expected (those who have ears to hear, let them hear because time is of the essence). I've heard many sermons that have satisfactorily encouraged and helped me greatly in my time of need and grievous dark days, but there's a statement that I still struggle with, and no preacher or teacher has truly explained it so that I understood: "Out of the mouth of infants and babes He ordained praise." The meaning of this simple yet profound statement became very clear in the most unexpected way and place; allow me to tell you the story of Fred the rooster.

I volunteered at my daughter's school (Orange Coast College, Harry & Grace Steele Children's Center in Costa Mesa, California) to help with their garden. At this wonderful school, they grow their own vegetables and other food items; they also raise farm animals such as chickens, goats, rabbits, roosters, etc. As I was clearing the weeds one day, I noticed a cross in the ground with "Freed" written on the horizontal arm.

1 believed whoever wrote this word on the cross truly understood the true meaning of forgiveness of sin and true heavenly salvation and rest. I was very impressed, and at the same time very intrigued, because this is not a Christian school. In my joy, I went to the director of the school, Susan Bierlich, to compliment her on such an amazing insight. It was then I was truly informed and educated as to what really happened, which was truly amazing and God-honoring. And there I found the satisfactory explanation to the above quoted scripture.

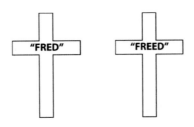

Susan Bierlich said that the cross was the children's idea and that what I saw was not "Freed" but "Fred." They had a rooster which the children named Fred. Unfortunately, Fred the rooster died, and all the children insisted that Fred must be given an honorable burial, so they (the children) dug a hole, placed Fred in the hole, and took turns covering Fred with the dirt. Afterward, they put a cross on Fred's grave with his name on the horizontal arm. Being from Africa, I greatly admire and stand in awe of these children, because in Africa the most honorable thing you can do for your loved ones that pass on to glory is to commit their bodies to the earth by first putting the dirt on them yourself (not the gardener or the mortuary staff—they can help finish). It's the most dignified thing one can do (those who have ears to hear, let them hear because time is of the essence). I had never known or heard of anyone giving such an honorable burial to a rooster. It was then I realized that truly out of the mouth of babes and infants God has ordained praise (Psalm 8:2; Matthew 21:16). These were children of many ethnicities and cultures; to see them play, laugh, cry, and fight together and immediately resume their friendships was an amazing sight to behold. This tells me that if children are raised in a godly environment, they will grow up as ordained by their Creator with less negative indoctrination by the parents. Yes, children are not born sinless; they do not arrive with a clean slate. Adamic blood runs through their veins as David clearly said: "Behold, I was brought forth in iniquity, and in sin my mother conceived me" (Psalm 51:5)—but we must do everything we can to lead them in the fear and admonition of the Lord (Ephesians 6:4). We either enhance their inherent sinful nature or instill in them an alternative as prescribed in the Scriptures. When we convolute their hearts and minds by what we do and say (or even by teaching them what is wrong), they become confused and gradually start to believe in our negative behavior and emulate us.

I once heard a story of an English man who came to the United States for a visit. Upon returning home, he was asked of his impression of the United States, to which he said, "In England we raise our children, but in the United States the children raise their parents." We must reverse this trend and lead them in the way they ought to be led. Remember: your children are not your friends; you must be friendly toward them, but do not make them your friends or best friends, as many parents have loudly and proudly proclaimed. The age difference alone disqualifies them from being your friends. They are your offspring, a blessing from God to be raised for His glory and their good. We must learn to be the students of our children. (Those who have ears to hear, let them hear because time is of the essence.)

There is a Chinese proverb that states, "The tree planted by the fathers in one generation will be beneficial to the children of the next generation for its shade." The question is, what type of trees are we planting for our children? When we are on our deathbed when our days are completed, will we be able to say like the apostle Paul, "I have fought the good fight, I have finished the race, I have kept the faith" (2 Timothy 4:7)? The good news is that it's never too late to amend our ways and start to live a life that will truly glorify God's name and edify our children. What we teach and encourage our children to embrace today will be their guiding light tomorrow. Their ideology and lifestyle today will become a law tomorrow. We need to bear in mind that the enemy of their soul (the devil) does not faint or get tired, but constantly refines his tools and is always on the lookout to catch them in their most vulnerable time and unguarded hour.

There's a lot we can learn from our children if we'll take the time to listen and observe them before we load their minds with erroneous doctrines without being aware of the danger we are putting them in. If we can humble ourselves as parents, listen and watch them, and pay closer attention to them, they have a lot to teach us about how simple life and living can be. The best legacy you and I can leave for the coming generations is godly offspring who will continue with the practice of godliness with contentment: "Now godliness with contentment is great gain" (1 Timothy 6:6).

It's my prayer that the Lord will continue to guide, uphold, and sustain us to raise our children for His honor and glory, and for their good.

Michael Abayomi Alabi
Isaiah 50:7

CHAPTER **ONE**

Day One

*O*nce upon a time, my dear child, in the beginning of time, a long, long time ago, while there was nothing but darkness, God in His infinite, immense, and divine power and wisdom decided to create the world. God said, "Let there be light" (Genesis 1:3–5; see also Psalm 33:9; 102:25), and immediately light appeared from His divine being. That light is within Him because He is the light of the whole world (John 1:9–11). He divided the light from the darkness; the light He called day, and the darkness He called night. This light is from Him and it's of Him because He is the light of the world (John 8:12), and He pronounced that it was good. There ended the first twenty-four hours of creation, my dear child—day one.

"The creation of Light"

CHAPTER **TWO**

Day Two

God, continuing with His creation, on day two said, "Let there be sky in the middle of the waters, and let it divide the waters" (see Genesis 1:6–8; Psalm 33:6). And behold, it was so immediately. God put one body of water over the sky and the other water below the sky. God called the sky heaven. Then God commanded the water below the sky to be in one place, and He commanded dry land to appear. Immediately, the water and the land obeyed the voice of God. God called the dry land earth, and the water He called sea. God pronounced that it was good. Then came the evening and the morning, the end of day two.

"The creation of the heavens"

CHAPTER **THREE**

Day Three

God said in the beginning of day three, "Let grass, and herb with seed, and fruit trees with fruit according to their kind with seeds, come from the earth" (see Genesis 1:11—13). The earth immediately obeyed the voice of God and brought forth grass, herb with seed, and fruit trees with seed, according to their kind. God pronounced that it was good; then came the evening and the morning, the end of day three.

"The creation of the sea and dry land with different kinds of vegetation; grass, herbs, fruit trees, etc"

CHAPTER **FOUR**

Day Four

Almighty God on day four said, "Let there be lights in the sky to divide the day from the night; and let them be for signs and seasons, for days and years. Let them be for lights in the sky to give light on the earth" (see Genesis 1:14–19; Psalm 74:16; 136:5–9). And immediately it was so; the lights obeyed the voice of God. Then God made two great lights, the greater light to rule the day (sun) and the lesser light to rule the night (moon). He also made the stars (Job 38:7; Psalm 19:1; Isaiah 40:26; Jeremiah 31:35). God put them in the sky to give light on the earth, to rule over the day and night, and to divide the light from darkness. God pronounced that it was good; then came the evening and the morning, the end of day four.

"The creation of the sun, moon and stars"

CHAPTER **FIVE**

Day Five

On the fifth day, God commanded the sea to be filled with all kinds of living things, according to their kind, and the sky to be filled with all varieties of birds. And immediately it was so. God also commanded the earth to be filled with animals and creeping things according to their kind, and immediately it was so (Genesis 1:20–25; Psalm 104:25–28). God looked and beheld that everything was good, and for the first time in His creation, God pronounced a blessing on them. He said, "Be fruitful and multiply, and fill the waters in the seas and let the birds multiply and fill the sky and the earth." God pronounced that everything was good. There ends the fifth day of creation.

"The creation of different kinds and types of sea creatures swimming in the sea. Many different kinds and types of winged flying birds"

CHAPTER **SIX**

Day Six

God saved the best for last, my dear, precious child. After God created everything that can sustain life and living, God created you, my dear, precious child. The three persons of the Trinity all agreed to create you in Their image and likeness (Genesis 1:26–31; 5:2). Remember, my precious child, from the first day of creation up to the fifth day, God spoke all His creation into being. When it came to you, He took His time to specially create you for Himself. He did not speak you into being, my precious child, and neither did you evolve (Psalm 100:3). Almighty God took His time to mold and shape your beautiful head with lovely eyes to behold and enjoy His lesser creations . . . your beautifully shaped nose to smell and enjoy everything He created for you . . . your perfectly shaped mouth with beautiful teeth to eat and enjoy food . . . your wonderful pair of ears to hear His call and the call of His other image bearers. He created your well-proportioned hands with lovely fingers to touch and enjoy the textures of your surroundings and the companionship of others . . . your lovely legs to move about and enjoy the feelings of your surroundings and to walk swiftly for His glory. You are fearfully and wonderfully made, my dear child (Psalm 139:13–14). He did something very, very special for you, my lovely child; He breathed life into you (Genesis 2:7), blessed you, and gave you authority over all His lesser creations (Genesis 1:29–30; 9:3; Psalm 104:14–15; 145:15–16)—something He had not done in His previous creation. He gave you everything created from the first day of creation to the fifth day. He created you to control, rule, and be in charge of them. But even more importantly, He created you to fellowship and have communion with Him and Him alone. After observing all His creation, He said what He had not said before with His previous creations. He pronounced, "It is very good" (see Genesis 1:31). What makes everything very good, my precious child, is you, the bearer of His image, the crown of His creation. There ends the sixth day of creation.

"The creation of Man"

CHAPTER **SEVEN**

Day Seven

*M*y precious child, on the seventh day (Sabbath or day of rest), God rested from all His work, and He blessed and sanctified it (Genesis 2:1–3). Since you are the bearer of God's image, He wants you, too, to rest from all your work and labor (fifth commandment; Exodus 20:8; Isaiah 58:13–14). Remember that God created the Sabbath (day of rest) for you; He did not create you for the Sabbath. This is the day God wants to specially meet with you and have your undivided attention as you worship, adore, and glorify His name (Isaiah 58:13–14).

"The Sabbath or day of rest"

Brief Overview

What was from the beginning?
- God (Genesis 1:1).
- Nothing but darkness (Genesis 1:2).
- The Spirit of God (Genesis 1:2).

Did God do something or say something in the beginning?
- God said something (Genesis 1:3).

What did God say?
- God said, "Let there be light" (Genesis 1:3).

What happened afterward?
- There was light immediately (Genesis 1:3).
- God saw that the light was good (Genesis 1:4).
- God separated the light from darkness (Genesis 1:4).
- He called the light day (Genesis 1:5).
- He called the darkness night (Genesis 1:5).
- That was the end of the first twenty-four hours of creation (Genesis 1:5).

What happened on the second day?

• God spoke the sky into existence to divide the waters. There was a body of water above the sky and one below (Genesis 1:7).

• God called the sky heaven (Genesis 1:8).

What happened on the third day?

• God separated the water from the dry land and commanded the earth to appear, and it appeared immediately (Genesis 1:9).

• God called the body of water the sea, and the dry land He called earth (Genesis 1:10).

• God filled the earth with vegetation (Genesis 1:11–13).

What happened on the fourth day?

• God created two great lights to rule the day and the night and to be signs, seasons, days, and years (Genesis 1:14–19).

What did God do on the fifth day?

• God filled the sea with abundant creatures, according to their kind. He also filled the sky with every winged bird (Genesis 1:20–21).

• God blessed them, saying, "Be fruitful and multiply, and fill the waters in the seas, and let birds multiply on the earth" (Genesis 1:22).

• God also filled the earth with living creatures, according to their kind (Genesis 1:24–25).

What happened on the sixth day?

• God created man and woman in His own image in agreement with the other two members of the Trinity: the Son Jesus Christ and the Holy Spirit (Genesis 1:26–27).

• God pronounced a blessing on them. He said, "Be fruitful and multiply; fill the earth and subdue it; have dominion over the fish of the sea, over the birds of the air, and over every living thing that moves on the earth" (Genesis 1:28).

- God personally gave man dominion over all His previous creations (Genesis 1:28–30).
- God saw everything that He made and pronounced it very good (Genesis 1:31).

What happened on the seventh day?
- God rested from all His work (Genesis 2:1–2).
- God blessed and sanctified the seventh day (Genesis 2:3).

For the Parents

I pray you and your children truly enjoyed reading *You Are Fearfully, Wonderfully, and Specially Made, My Child-The Beginning.* The following biblical passages are designed to further develop and stimulate their minds by guiding and inspiring them to take an interest in the Scriptures, not as a chore to impress you, but as a lifestyle.

If these questions and concepts are too advanced for your child now, you can always return to them later as they grow in God's grace. As you prayerfully read these passages with them, go at their pace. Be mindful of their state of mind; read this section at a time when they are apt to enjoy and retain the information. While reading with them, make it fun. It's not supposed to be a chore or an assignment. At the same time, let them know that it is a very important and serious matter.

> Discretion will preserve you; understanding
> will keep you, to deliver you from the
> way of evil, from the man who speaks
> perverse things. (Proverbs 2:11–12)

Honor your father and your mother, that your days may be long upon the land which the LORD your God is giving you. (Exodus 20:12)

My son, if you receive my words, and treasure my commands within you, so that you incline your ear to wisdom, and apply your heart to understanding; yes, if you cry out for discernment, and lift up your voice for understanding, if you seek her as silver, and search for her as for hidden treasures; then you will understand the fear of the LORD, and find the knowledge of God. (Proverbs 2:1–5)

My son, give attention to my words; incline your ear to my sayings. Do not let them depart from your eyes; keep them in the midst of your heart; for they are life to those who find them, and health to all their flesh. Keep your heart with all diligence, for out of it spring the issues of life. Put away from you a deceitful mouth, and put perverse lips far from you. Let your eyes look straight ahead, and your eyelids look right before you. Ponder the path of your feet, and let all your ways be established. Do not turn to the right or the left; remove your foot from evil. (Proverbs 4:20–27)

He who spares his rod hates his son,
but he who loves him disciplines
him promptly. (Proverbs 13:24)

Better is the poor who walks in his
integrity than one who is perverse in his
lips, and is a fool. (Proverbs 19:1)

Whoever curses his father or his mother, his lamp
will be put out in deep darkness. (Proverbs 20:20)

Make no friendship with an angry man, and with
a furious man do not go, lest you learn his ways
and set a snare for your soul. (Proverbs 22:24–25)

Do not be envious of evil men, nor desire
to be with them. (Proverbs 24:1)

Better is the poor who walks in his integrity
than one perverse in his ways, though
he be rich. Whoever keeps the law is a
discerning son, but a companion of gluttons
shames his father. (Proverbs 28:6–7)

The fear of man brings a snare, but whoever trusts in the LORD shall be safe. (Proverbs 29:25)

Two things I request of You (deprive me not before I die): Remove falsehood and lies far from me; give me neither poverty nor riches— feed me with the food allotted to me; lest I be full and deny You, and say, "Who is the LORD?" or lest I be poor and steal, and profane the name of my God. (Proverbs 30:7–9)

But Jesus said, "Let the little children come to Me, and do not forbid them; for of such is the kingdom of heaven." (Matthew 19:14)

Children, obey your parents in the Lord, for this is right. (Ephesians 6:1)

Behold, children are a heritage from the LORD, the fruit of the womb is a reward. Like arrows in the hand of a warrior, so are the children of one's youth. Happy is the man who has his quiver full of them; they shall not be ashamed, but shall speak with their enemies in the gate. (Psalm 127:3–5)

In Conclusion

In conclusion, my child, who are you? This is a question of identity; by asking who you are I'm not referring to what you do, it's my prayer that the Lord will bless any venture He has gifted you with, so that you can be a blessing to your family, to those who are in need, and also to the Lord.) Your identity is wrapped up in your Creator from the genesis of your life. This is who you are, my child, this is your true identity. You are the bearer of God's image (Genesis 1:26), a sinner (Genesis 3:1–13), saved by God's grace and His grace alone (Genesis 3:15).

- **The bearer of God's image:** Remember our triune God's statement after everything had been made by speaking it into existence: "Let Us make man in Our image, according to Our likeness" (Genesis 1:26). Bear in mind, my dear child, God did not speak you into existence. His love for you is so great that He took His time to create you to bear His image. This is your first and foremost identity, my dear child; do not forget it. You are very precious to God; you bear His image. Bear that image graciously for your good and His glory.
- **A sinner:** Yes, God's love for you is beyond any other love in the world, but you are a sinner, my precious child. You

are not a sinner because you sin; you sin because you are a sinner. We all inherited the sin of our federal head Adam and Eve (Genesis 3:1–13; Psalm 51:5; Romans 3:9–18). My dear child, Adamic blood runs through your veins because he represented you before God right from the beginning of time.

- **Saved by grace:** Despite your sinfulness and sinful nature, my child, despite the fact that God promised that the end result of sin is death—(that is, physical and spiritual separation from Him (Genesis 2:16–17)—God's grace, mercy, compassion, and loving-kindness caught up with His justice and brought you His mercy and grace instead of His justice—which we all do rightly deserve (Psalm 103:1–5; Isaiah 53:4–5). Yes, our federal head Adam and Eve died immediately (spiritually), whereby God was separated from them, but God in His infinite mercy made a way of escape for them—and for us by extension, whereby we are restored back to Him spiritually (Genesis 3:15; Psalm 22; Matthew 27:45–54; Mark 15:33–34; Luke 23:44–47; John 19:28–30). Remember, my child, God owned you twice. He owned you by creating you; He also owned you by redeeming you. You are His and His alone in your entirety.

Since God already provided a way of salvation for you, the next question then is, why are you saved, my child? From who or what—and for what purpose—are you saved? As the psalmist rightly declared, "Salvation belongs to the LORD" (Psalm 3:8).

- **Why are you saved?** According to Pastor R.C. Sproul, salvation, by definition, is "a saving, or being saved from danger, evil, difficulty or destruction; deliverance from sin and the penalties of sin." There are four kinds of people in the world. There are people who are saved, and they know that they are saved. There are people who are saved, and they do not know that they are saved. There are people who are not saved, and they know that they are not saved. There are people who are not saved but wholeheartedly believe that they are saved. It's my prayer that you will have the definite assurance of your salvation, my child, and that your salvation will not rest on what you do, but what our great Savior Jesus Christ has done for you in His birth, life, death, and resurrection. You are saved to proclaim the glory of God in your salvation (Jeremiah 31:2–14)[3]

- **From whom or what are you saved?** Pastor R.C. Sproul further said that "we are being saved by God from God." Yes, my dear child, God is a great, loving, long-suffering, and compassionate God in all His attributes, but He's also a vengeful, just, and destructive God who will not overlook sin or wink at iniquities. It is God who will one day bring down His justice on all His enemies by destroying their bodies and souls in hell for eternity (Psalm 28:5; 52:5; 101:8; Matthew 10:28). He will not send their sin to hell, but will send the sinners with their sin and iniquities to eternal hell.[4]

A Letter to My Daughter and a Lesson Learned

My dear Sade,

As I'm writing this letter to you, I'm filled with so many emotions, and it's very overwhelming. It was like yesterday when I first saw you. Your delicate, sincere, helpless, kind, adorable, fragile, gentle, and tender look spoke so much to my heart. I was so thrilled and joyful, and felt extremely blessed to know that you were my daughter. At the same time, I was filled with so much fear, helplessness, anxiety, and awe because of your fragility and helpless look—and because of the fact that you'll be growing up in a dangerous, sinful, and destructive world. I turned to God immediately and said a quick prayer for you, your mom, and myself because I know from whom my help comes (Psalm 121:1–2). Your mom was so happy and extremely thrilled for you also.

To see you begin life and living is truly an amazing grace. All the odds that are stacked against you are beaten by grace, God's grace alone.

To see you crawl, climb, jump, run, chew, reach out to be carried, and progressively grow in God's grace was just amazingly profound. For me and your mom to be able to change your diaper, bathe you, clean you, carry you, put you to sleep, sing to you, listen to your silly babbling and singing; to see you dressing your-self, wearing your mother's shoes, trying to mimic her; to see your resilience and strong-willed nature, your love for laughter and for hiding under the bed when you wanted to use the bathroom, your decency and many other behaviors you exhibited . . . to see you clasp your hands when it was time for prayer before our meals (you were even able to say the simple table grace after us—"God is good, God is great, and we thank Him for this food; bow our heads, we are fed, thank You, Lord, for daily bread, in Jesus' name—Amen") . . . to see you clasp your hands during the morning and evening prayers (able to say and even sign, "Jesus loves me, this I know") fills my soul with so much delight, joy, and thankfulness to God.

As I was thinking about you, wondering what legacy I want to leave for you and for your future, I did not think long before I came to the conclusion that the best legacy I can leave for you is that which was left for me by my maternal grandmother, your great-grandmother: the legacy of "godliness with contentment" (1 Timothy 6:6). I want you to be satisfied in the Lord first and fore-most; you will not have everything you want or crave in life, but be self-sufficient. Don't allow your external circumstances to dictate your internal sufficiency. Learn how to live with plenty and how to live with little (Philippians 4:12). The Lord will never leave you nor forsake you (Psalm 27:9). Remember that God is the source of true contentment; be satisfied in Him alone. He has given you your greatest need—Christ; He will give you your lesser needs. As you journey through life and living, my dear, precious child, there are ten things I want you to know for sure and constantly bear in mind as long as you shall live. (This is not exhaustive, my child.)

1. **Prayer, prayer, and prayer.** The apostle Paul simply said, "Pray without ceasing" (1 Thessalonians 5:17). Prayer is your walking stick, with which you walk with Christ the Lord, my dear child. Your whole Christian journey depends on your prayer life. You do not pray

only when things are bad, when everything you hold dear and near to your heart goes down the drain, but also when things are going in your favor, the way you planned. A Christian that cannot pray is a cheap target for the evil one. Make prayer the chief cornerstone of your life; your whole existence depends on it. Prayer is your walking stick with which you walk with Christ the Lord (Matthew 21:22; Philippians 4:6–7; 1 Thessalonians 5:16–17).

2. **Jesus loves you, this I know.** Yes, I do love you, my dear child, but God's love for you is far beyond my love for you, ad infinitum. As you already see and know from creation, God loves you so much that He took His time to create rather than speak you into existence as He did other creations. His love for you is beyond my understanding; it's beyond human understanding because we cannot comprehend the depth or breadth of His love. His love is a strange love because He loved you so much that He died for you (Matthew 19:13–15; Mark 10:13–16; Luke 18:15–17).

3. **Bad company corrupts good manners.** My dear child, don't associate with shady and godless characters. Don't move in their crowd, and don't co-mingle your affairs with theirs because they will draw your heart away, in a subtle manner, from your God. Remember that everything that shines is not gold. They will present you with what appears to be good and pleasurable, but this pleasure is not pleasure that will last for eternity; it's an earthly pleasure that will soon pass away—and, in its place, misery will last for eternity (Psalm 1:1–2; Proverbs 13:20; 25:26; 28:7; 1 Corinthians 15:33–34). I pray you will not learn this amazing lesson the way I did: the hard way. (Carefully read "A Lesson Learned.")

4. **You bear God's image; bear it to His glory.** Remember what God said concerning you before you were created: "Let Us make man in Our image" (Genesis 1:26). God loves you so much that He gave you the breath of life. The image you bear both intrinsically and extrinsically is not that of an animal or of an inanimate object. So bear the image of God graciously to His glory, because you did not evolve as so many would like you to believe; rather, your heavenly Father made you to fellowship with you, and to also fellowship with other bearers of His image. You are to be aware of His image (both intrinsic and extrinsic) by being aware of your body, mind, and soul. What you wear, what you say, and the company you keep will ultimately reflect God's image (1 Timothy 2:9–10; 1 Peter 3:3–6).

5. **Be strong and courageous, my child.** It's my prayer that I'll live long enough to guide and lead you in the fear and admonition of the Lord, from where strength and courage are derived (this is my responsibility to you and a commandment from the Lord), but if not, I know for a fact that the Lord will always guide, uphold, and sustain you for the glory of His name and for your good. But you must be strong and courageous in the Lord, my precious child (Joshua 1:8–9; Psalm 27:14; 31:2, 24). Commit your ways to His care, and do not be afraid. His strength will continuously guide you (Isaiah 41:10). Do not depend on the arms of flesh for strength or courage but in the Lord alone (Psalm 71:3, 7–8; 2 Timothy 2:1). That's why you must put on the whole armor of God always, for in Him alone you'll stand, and stand to the end (Ephesians 6:10–13).

6. **Seek the Lord while He may be found.** Today is your day of salvation, my precious child. Tomorrow is not

promised to you. I know that the worries and cares of life can sometimes seems to eclipse God's love, but you must fight the good fight of faith as a good soldier of the Lord. The battle will rage in your heart and mind, but be reminded that the more you rest your mind on Him, the more He will carry you through (Psalm 32:6; Isaiah 26:3–4). Remember that the Lord is always near to you. Remember that you are prone to wander away and leave the God you love and who loves you. Guard against this temptation very carefully, and He will aid you. Be reminded of Horatio R. Palmer's refrain of the song titled "Yield Not to Temptation": "Ask the Savior to help you, comfort, strengthen, and keep you. He is willing to aid you, He will carry you through."

7. **Always remember who you are and whose you are.** Remember, my dear, precious child, you belong to this family. The one thing we hold dear and near is our reputation as a Christian family. You will not be perfect, but you must not compromise your stand as a Christian. Also, be aware whose you are. You belong to the Lord. Be mindful of the name you bear: "Christian." It's a blood-bought name. Don't let Calvary be far from your heart and mind. Remember that all those who name the name of the Lord must depart from iniquity (2 Timothy 2:19). Don't let indifference stifle or smother the Word of God in your heart.

8. **Don't be overly troubled by tribulations, and don't be overly carried away by success.** I don't want you to be ignorant of the fact that, as a Christian, you'll go through some hard times; that's part of your call-ing. You are living in a world ruled by the devil; this is not your home. This world is not your own—you are a sojourner. Don't get so comfortable that you forget

your eternal home. Be reminded of Jonathan Edwards's statement: "No person who seeks to go on a pilgrimage to a glorious and exotic place will take up permanent residence at an inn along the way. Christians who cling tenaciously to this world and to this life are like sojourners who get stuck in a wayside inn, having lost sight of their glorious destination." This world is not your own. You're just passing through. Also, be reminded of the Word of our Lord and Savior: "In the world you will have tribulation" (John 16:33) and of the apostle Peter's admonition: "Don't think that it's strange that you go through trials and tribulation" (see 1 Peter 4:12–13). It's my prayer that the Lord will grant me enough time to guide and lead you to a point whereby you'll be strong enough to stand firm, but if not be assured that God's grace will continuously guide, uphold, and sustain you. Remember that you can only live right when you think right.

9. **Have discernment.** Ask the Lord for discernment, my dear, precious child; you'll be growing up in a world totally different from the world I grew up in. Your world is more troubling and more anti-God, hence you need to be very discerning, my precious child (Ecclesiastes 8:5). Remember that right thinking can only lead to right living. Don't yield your mind to every fable and doctrine that comes your way. Don't believe everything you hear. Do your due diligence and be very prayerful (Malachi 3:18). Be noble as the Bereans by searching the Scriptures to approve or disapprove of everything you hear (Acts 17:10–11). Be quick to hear but slow with your response (Proverbs 10:19; 17:27; James 1:19).

10. **Worship the Lord with your heart; evangelize the lost by your life.** Remember that God created you to

fellowship with you. Worship Him and Him alone with your heart. He alone deserves your highest adoration and worship. Worship Him in Spirit and truth (Deuteronomy 30:6; John 4:24; Romans 2:28–29). Remember that evangelizing the world around you is a commandment of the Lord Himself (1 Chronicles 16:23; Matthew 28:18–20; Acts 1:8). Even though this commandment was given directly to His apostles, by extension He gave you the same commandment. Be mindful that as a Christian lady, you evangelize the world around you every day by what you say and what you don't say; by where you go and where you don't go; and by the company you keep and the company you don't keep. Don't let your testimony be corrupted or marred by what you say or do, or by the company you keep. You "advertise" the Lord every day; advertise Him well, my dear child.

It's been my huge privilege, and still is my utmost privilege, to be your father. It's one of the greatest joys and blessings of my life. You've brought me unspeakable moments of joy I never thought existed. I commend you to the care of our heavenly Father, who is able to keep you from stumbling and to present you faultless before the throne of His glory with exceeding joy now and forever more (2 Timothy 1:2; Jude 24).

Your loving and grateful father,
Michael Abayomi Alabi
Isaiah 50:7

P.S.: **A lesson Learned**
Even though I was raised in a Christian home by my loving and faithful maternal grandmother who poured her life into mine, I still erred in my ways while I was growing up. (That fact that I was raised in a Christian home does not make me a Christian, and

growing up in a Christian home will not make you a Christian either. Read and be familiar with the children of Eli the priest and the children of Samuel.) I will always remember and praise the Lord for my high school principal, Rev. (Dr.) Adegbite of Lagos Baptist Academy in Lagos, Nigeria, whose words of wisdom I still bear in mind today. He was truly one of God's conduits of grace for my growth in His grace.

While in school, I tried so much to fit in with a group of my fellow students whose character was ungodly and very shady. Because they were popular and well-liked by everyone, and because they appeared to be trendy and always in the know, I tried so hard to fit in their group. One day while school was in session, we all decided to sneak out of school to go to a football game with the hope that we could also sneak back in unnoticed. As we were sneaking back in, the gate man of the school noticed us and informed the other guards, who ran after us. Fortunately and unfortunately, I was the only one apprehended; the others ran away. The gate man took me immediately to the principal's office to report what had happened. In my days, when you were taken to the principal's office, it was either for a very good cause or for a very serious cause, which mostly resulted either in praise or with serious punishment. As you probably have figured out, my trip resulted in the latter of the two. Dr. Adegbite (the principal) knew that I came from a Christian family, so hearing what happened truly troubled and surprised him greatly.

After the gate man left, Dr. Adegbite asked me to sit down. This was truly unheard of and made me uncomfortable because when you went to the principal's office to be punished, you stood up until you received your punishment; you never sat down. He saw my discomfort and how hard it was for me to sit down in his presence. After I finally sat down, he turned to me, and the following conversation ensued.

The Principal: Why did you choose to sneak out of school?

Me: No response.

The Principal: Where did you all go to?

Me: No response.

The principal: How many of you students sneaked out?

Me: No response.

The Principal: Where are all your other friends now?

Me: No response.

The Principal: I want you to listen to me very carefully, and remember what I'm going to tell you for the rest of your life. I know that you come from a Christian home. You always do very well in Bible studies and always attend the Scripture Union (SU), but you failed to realize that bad company always corrupts good manners (1 Corinthians 15:33). You forgot who you are and whose you are. All your friends ran away, and you are now alone standing before me. Remember that in the last day, so it will be when you stand before God all alone. Your friends will not and can not stand with you or for you. They will stand for themselves before God as you are now standing before me—all alone. On that day, the only advocate you'll need is Christ and Him alone. If you don't know Him and fellowship with Him while you are living, it will be too late then. Son, do not move in the company of lawless students. Make sure that you always look before you leap. Think before you act, son, and don't allow yourself to just go with the flow. The flow will always lead you to where you don't belong. You can go to your class now.

This interaction with my principal taught me a great lesson and shook me up so much that I wept after leaving his office. The pain and reality of his statement brought me face-to-face with my sinful nature and tendency for sinful deeds. If I'd had my choice, I would rather have had him flog me than speak to me the way he did. I thank God that I didn't have that privilege or choice. His words still resonate with me even after forty years. My principal taught me a lesson of a lifetime. He taught me that Christianity is not a name you have but a lifestyle to be lived out privately and publicly for all to know and see. My precious child, you don't have to say that you are a Christian for the world around you to know that you dance to a different beat; you belong to Christ and Him alone.

It's my prayer that you'll learn from other people's mistakes, my dear child, especially your father's, because you'll not live long enough to make them all, and it will be well with you.

After the death of your brother Akin (the warrior), I wrote a poem for your mother which has truly brought us immense hope even in the face of severe trial and tribulation. I pray this poem will bring you as much joy and hope in your days of trial and tribulation as it has brought me and your mother in our time of need. It is titled "My Grace Is Sufficient for You."

My Grace Is Sufficient for You

2 Corinthians 12:9

1

When your light turns into darkness,
When your joy becomes sorrow,
When your hope becomes despair
And your laughter turns into weeping,
So He gently says, "My grace is sufficient for you."

2

When your friends become foes,
When love turns into hatred,
When pleasure becomes a burden,
When sweetness turns into bitterness,
So He gently says, "My grace is sufficient for you."

3

When your journey is long and unknown,
When there is no direction or map to follow,
When the compass becomes the enemy,
When your body, mind, and soul become weary and tired,
So He gently says, "My grace is sufficient for you."

4

When the hands of death thy life clutch,
When the angel of death lay at thy bosom,
When the taste of death thy mouth fills,
When the smell of death thy nostrils fills,
So He gently says, "Even then My grace is sufficient for you."

HELPFUL RESOURCES FOR FURTHER READING

Beeke, Joel. *God's Alphabet for Life: Devotions for Young Children*
— *Parenting by God's Promises: How to Raise Children in the Covenant of Grace*
Boekestein, William. *Faithfulness Under Fire: The Story of Guido de Bres*
Carr, Simonetta. *Athanasius (Christian Biographies for Young Readers)*
— *Augustine of Hippo (Christian Biographies for Young Readers)*
— *John Calvin (Christian Biographies for Young Readers)*
— *John Owen (Christian Biographies for Young Readers)*
Ferguson, Dr. Sinclair. *The Big Book of Questions & Answers About Jesus*
— *The Magnificent Amazing Time Machine: A Journey Back to the Cross*
Ferguson, Dr. Sinclair and Alison Brown. *Ignatius of Antioch (Heroes of the Faith)*
— *Iranaeus of Lyons (Heroes of the Faith)*
— *Polycarp of Smyrna (Heroes of the Faith)*
Hunt, Susan. *Sammy and His Shepherd: Seeing Jesus in Psalm 23*
Nichols, Stephen J. and Ned Bustard. *The Church History ABCs*

MacArthur, John. *A Faith to Grow On*

— *Being a Dad Who Leads*

— *Right Thinking in a World Gone Wrong: A Biblical Response to Today's Most Controversial Issues*

MacArthur, John and Pam Rossi. *I Believe in Jesus: Leading Your Child to Christ*

Sproul, Denise and Carol DeMar. *Tending Your Garden: Wisdom for Keepers at Home*

Sproul, R.C. *The Donkey Who Carried a King*

Sproul, R.C., Greg Bailey, and Justin Gerard. *The Priest with Dirty Clothes*

Sproul, R.C. and Justin Gerard. *The Lightlings*

— *The Prince's Poison Cup*

Sproul, R.C. and Liz Bonham. *The King Without a Shadow*

Sproul, R.C. and T. Lively Fluharty. *The Barber Who Wanted to Pray*

Tripp, Tedd. *Shepherding a Child's Heart*

SYNOPSIS

Children are the weakest, most fragile, most gullible, and most naïve; and their naiveté can be easily exploited by the unscrupulous men and women in society who take advantage of them in the earliest years of their lives. Once their minds are captured and encumbered with negative and un-Christlike influences at this crucial time in their lives, it's very hard to realign them and set them on the path of righteousness again. Hence, they need to be influenced for Christ from the genesis of their lives. They need to be reminded that they live in the world but they are not of the world.

You Are Fearfully, Wonderfully, and Specially Made, My Child: The Beginning is written with this in mind and takes a careful look at our society and the deadly influences some media have on the hearts and minds of the children—and what we must do as parents (especially the fathers) to combat this negative indoctrination.

BIBLIOGRAPHY

1. MacArthur, John: *Right Thinking in a World Gone Wrong:* Oregon: Harvest House, 2009.
2. Carter, Joe: Table Talk Magazine: http://www.ligonier.org/learn/articles/defining-marriage
3. Sproul, R.C.: Renewing Your Mind broadcast: http://www.oneplace.com/ministries/renewing-your-mind/
4. Sproul, R.C.: Renewing Your Mind broadcast: http://www.oneplace.com/ministries/renewing-your-mind/

ABOUT THE AUTHOR

 Michael A. Alabi is a native of Nigeria, West Africa. He obtained his primary education at Lagos Baptist Academy in Lagos, Nigeria. He immigrated to the United States in 1983. He obtained his Nursing license from Casa Loma College in Lake View Terrace, California. He later obtained his Bachelor of Science degree in Accounting from California State University, Northridge, California. He currently lives in Southern California with his daughter.

Made in the USA
Middletown, DE
06 November 2021